Animal Engineers
PRAIRIE DOG BURROWS

by Christopher Forest

D0521451

FOCUS
READERS

FOCUS READERS

www.focusreaders.com

Focus Readers is distributed by North Star Editions:
sales@northstareditions.com | 888-417-0195

Produced for Focus Readers by Red Line Editorial.

Photographs ©: Andyworks/iStockphoto, cover, 1; Dlogger/Shutterstock Images, 4–5; AlessandroZocc/Shutterstock Images, 6; scigelova/iStockphoto, 8–9; Arina P Habich/ Shutterstock Images, 11; Zoltan Tarlacz/Shutterstock Images, 13; SochAnam/iStockphoto, 14–15, 29; Henk Bentlage/Shutterstock Images, 16–17; Gregory Johnston/Shutterstock Images, 19; Eric Gevaert/Shutterstock Images, 21; David Butler/iStockphoto, 22–23; Lynn Wild/Shutterstock Images, 25; Kerry Hargrove/Shutterstock Images, 27

ISBN
978-1-63517-862-3 (hardcover)
978-1-63517-963-7 (paperback)
978-1-64185-166-4 (ebook pdf)
978-1-64185-065-0 (hosted ebook)

Library of Congress Control Number: 2018931113

Printed in the United States of America
Mankato, MN
May, 2018

About the Author

Christopher Forest is a middle school teacher in Massachusetts. He has written stories, articles, and novels for readers of all ages. In his spare time, he enjoys watching sports, playing guitar, reading, and spending time outdoors.

TABLE OF CONTENTS

CHAPTER 1

SAFE UNDERGROUND

Four prairie dogs nibble a patch of grass. Suddenly, one lifts his head. He senses danger. A coyote is near. The prairie dog squeaks to warn the others. Together, they dash toward a **mound** of dirt.

> **Prairie dogs leave their burrow to look for food.**

A prairie dog looks out from its burrow.

The mound has a hole on top. The prairie dogs scurry inside it. The hole is an entrance to their burrow. Three of the prairie dogs huddle

6

inside. The fourth stands by the entrance. He lets the others know when it is safe to come out.

Prairie dogs live in underground homes called burrows. The burrows are made of many tunnels and **chambers**. A burrow helps prairie dogs hide. It keeps them safe from **predators**.

FUN FACT

Some prairie dog burrows go more than 10 feet (3.0 m) underground.

CHAPTER 2

DIGGING IN THE DIRT

Prairie dogs make burrows in flat, grassy areas. They start by digging a hole in the ground. The hole is 4 to 8 inches (10 to 20 cm) wide. It is the exit and entrance to the burrow.

▷ **Prairie dogs use their front paws to dig.**

Below the hole, the prairie dogs dig tunnels. Some tunnels lead to chambers. Others go back up to the surface. These tunnels result in more entrance or exit holes.

As prairie dogs dig, dirt comes loose. They move the dirt outside the burrow's hole. The dirt piles up. A mound forms. The mound

FUN FACT

The tunnels in a burrow can be more than 20 feet (6.1 m) long.

A prairie dog stands near an exit hole.

protects the burrow from floods. Its sides keep water from flowing into the tunnels.

Prairie dogs use their noses to push dirt along the tunnel's sides.

They pack the dirt tightly so it stays firm against the walls. Sometimes dirt falls down from the walls. It blocks the tunnel. The prairie dogs dig quickly to clear it.

Prairie dogs live in small groups called coteries. A prairie dog coterie is like a family. It includes a male, two to eight females, and their **pups**. Each coterie has its own burrow.

Several coteries often live together as a **colony**. They dig

> **A colony of prairie dogs can make many mounds.**

their burrows close together. The burrows might even be connected by tunnels. A colony can include up to 50 burrows.

HOLES FOR AIRFLOW

Each prairie dog burrow has at least two holes that reach the surface. The holes are entrances and exits. They also help with **ventilation**. Prairie dog burrows are underground, so they tend be warm. Smells can easily build up inside. But the two holes keep air moving through the burrow.

One hole is usually located on higher ground. Wind moves faster over this hole, causing a difference in air pressure at the two exits. As a result, air flows into the lower hole. The air is sucked through the burrow. Then it leaves through the higher hole.

A prairie dog guards the entrance to its burrow.

CHAPTER 3

PRAIRIE DOG FAMILIES

Each prairie dog burrow has several chambers. Prairie dogs use some chambers for sleeping. They build nests in these chambers. At least one chamber is a **nursery**. It holds the prairie dog pups.

Prairie dog pups are born inside the burrow.

Prairie dog pups are born in the spring or summer. Their parents care for them. The pups stay inside the burrow until they are six weeks old.

Prairie dogs spend nights in their burrows. But they are active during the day. In the morning and early evening, they go out to look for food.

Prairie dogs leave the burrow in small groups. A few prairie dogs stay behind. They stand on the

 **A prairie dog stands and squeaks when it senses danger.**

mounds near the exit holes. They

look and listen for signs of danger.

Prairie dogs take turns listening.

If danger is close, they let out a high-pitched bark. This alerts the others. They scurry back to the burrow. There, they will be safe.

Prairie dogs eat grasses, roots, and weeds. Sometimes they eat insects. They also trim grass and small plants near the mounds. This makes it easier to see predators.

FUN FACT

Most burrows have a chamber that prairie dogs use as a bathroom.

 Prairie dogs carry grass to their burrows to make nests.

The prairie dogs keep the grass and plants. They bring the pieces into their burrow. They line the chambers to make nests.

CHAPTER 4

BURROW EFFECTS

Prairie dogs affect the area around them in many ways. A prairie dog colony can cover a large amount of land. Prairie dogs can create problems for farms. Their holes can make farmland **unstable**.

Prairie dogs can fill a field with tunnels and holes.

Livestock such as horses and cattle can fall into the holes.

As prairie dogs dig, they may eat the roots of plants. This hurts the plants. It can harm crops growing on farms. Plus, prairie dogs eat the grass around their burrows.

FUN FACT

A group of prairie dogs can dig 50 to 60 holes in 1 acre (0.4 hectares) of land.

 Many farmers and ranchers try to get rid of the prairie dogs on their land.

That means there is less grass for

the farm animals to eat.

But prairie dogs also help the **environment**. As they dig holes, they might rip up shrubs that are crowding out other plants. Without the shrubs, there is more room for plants to grow.

Prairie dog burrows can help other animals, too. Some animals

FUN FACT

The largest prairie dog colony ever found stretched for 25,000 square miles (65,000 sq km). Scientists think that 400 million prairie dogs lived inside it.

▷ **Black-footed ferrets sometimes make homes in prairie dog burrows.**

take over **abandoned** burrows.
These include rattlesnakes and
ground-burrowing owls. Thanks
to prairie dogs, these animals
have homes.

FOCUS ON
PRAIRIE DOG BURROWS

Write your answers on a separate piece of paper.

1. Write a paragraph describing how prairie dog burrows affect the land around them.

2. If you were a farmer, would you want prairie dogs on your land? Why or why not?

3. What part of their burrows do prairie dogs stand on to watch for danger?
- A. the chambers
- B. the mounds
- C. the tunnels

4. Why do prairie dogs look for food in groups?
- A. so they can blend in with their habitat
- B. so they do not get lonely
- C. so they can better watch out for predators

5. What does the word **huddle** mean in this book?

*The hole is an entrance to their burrow. Three of the prairie dogs **huddle** inside.*

 A. cry loudly
 B. dig in the dirt
 C. gather together

6. What does the word **livestock** mean in this book?

*Their holes can make farmland unstable. **Livestock** such as horses and cattle can fall into the holes.*

 A. animals that are raised on a farm
 B. tools that are used to plant seeds
 C. people who take care of animals

Answer key on page 32.

GLOSSARY

abandoned
Left behind or no longer used.

chambers
Spaces used as rooms.

colony
A group of animals that live together.

environment
The natural surroundings of living things in a particular place.

mound
A hill or pile.

nursery
A place where babies are kept.

predators
Animals that hunt other animals for food.

pups
Babies or young prairie dogs.

unstable
Likely to move, change, or fall apart.

ventilation
The process of bringing in fresh air and removing stale air.

TO LEARN MORE

BOOKS

Gray, Leon. *Amazing Animal Engineers*. North Mankato, MN: Capstone Press, 2016.

Grucella, A. J. *Prairie Dogs in Danger*. New York: Gareth Stevens Publishing, 2014.

Roth, Susan L., and Cindy Trumbore. *Prairie Dog Song: The Key to Saving North America's Grasslands*. New York: Lee & Low Books, 2016.

NOTE TO EDUCATORS

Visit **www.focusreaders.com** to find lesson plans, activities, links, and other resources related to this title.

INDEX

Answer Key: 1. Answers will vary; **2.** Answers will vary; **3.** B; **4.** C; **5.** C; **6.** A